# Team Stats—Football Edition

# HIGHLIGHTS OF THE SEATTLE SEAHAWKS

## MARYSA STORM

BLACK
RABBIT
BOOKS

Bolt is published by Black Rabbit Books
P.O. Box 3263, Mankato, Minnesota, 56002.
www.blackrabbitbooks.com
Copyright © 2020 Black Rabbit Books

Jennifer Besel, editor; Michael Sellner, interior
designer; Grant Gould, cover designer; Omay
Ayres, photo researcher

Cataloging-in-Publication Data is available at the Library of Congress.
ISBN 978-1-68072-889-7 (library binding)
ISBN 978-1-68072-895-8 (e-book)
ISBN 978-1-64466-086-7 (paperback)

Printed in the United States of America. 1/19

## Image Credits
Alamy: Xinhua, 8; AP Images:
Elaine Thompson, 25; G. Newman
Lowrance, 18 (bkgd); Greg Trott, 15; NFL/ LI-
EBB, 7, 22 (m); Paul Abell, 12–13; Ted S. Warren,
1;vReed, 20; Getty: Gene Lower, 3, 16–17 (bkgd);
George Gojkovich, 23 (r); Miguel A. Elliot, 27; Otto
Greule Jr, 16–17 (Alexander); Sporting News, 28–29 (b);
Newscom: David Gonzales 787, 18–19; Dean J. Koepfler/
Tacoma News Tribune, 22 (r; Elsa Hasch/TSN/Icon SMI,
23 (l); Michael Zito, 19; Robin Alam/Icon Sportswire, 22
(l); Sean Gardner, 4–5; Shutterstock: EFKS, 22–23 (bkgd);
enterlinedesign, 28–29 (t); Orgus88, 24; Svyatoslav Alek-
sandrov, 31; VitaminCo, 10–11 (ball), 20, 32; Superstock:
Cooper, Ed, 11 (main); USA Today Sports: Joe Nichol-
son, Cover
Every effort has been made to contact copyright
holders for material reproduced in this
book. Any omissions will be rectified in
subsequent printings if notice is
given to the publisher.

# CONTENTS

# CHAPTER 1

# On the FIELD

It was the 2010 season **playoffs**. The Seattle Seahawks faced the New Orleans Saints. During the game, Seahawks running back Marshawn Lynch got the ball. He took off. Several Saints nearly took him down. But Lynch escaped. He charged down the field. He pushed away a **defender**. Then he nearly went out of bounds to miss another. The 67-yard run ended with a touchdown. Players and fans went wild!

# of the Seahawks

The Seahawks started playing in 1976. The team only won two games its first season. But Seahawks players and fans were still excited. They were just happy to have a pro football team.

In 1984, the team **retired** number 12 to honor its fans.

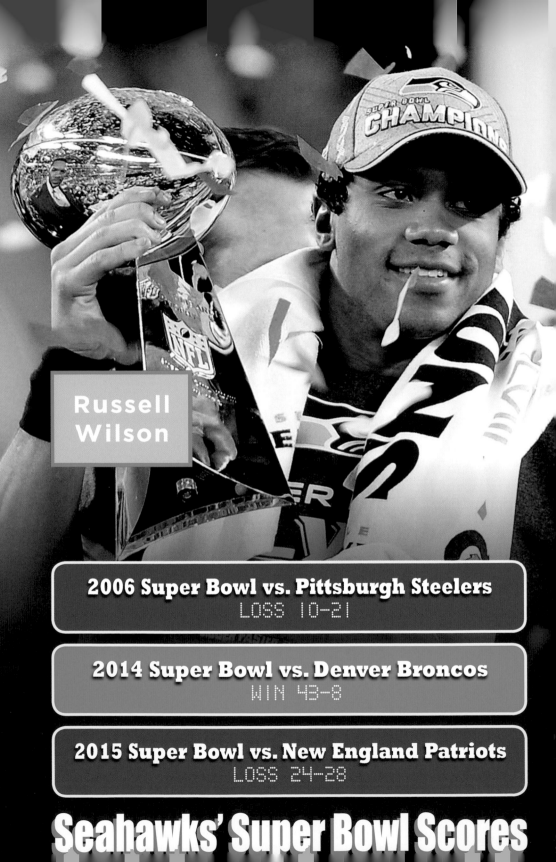

Russell Wilson

**2006 Super Bowl vs. Pittsburgh Steelers**
LOSS 10-21

**2014 Super Bowl vs. Denver Broncos**
WIN 43-8

**2015 Super Bowl vs. New England Patriots**
LOSS 24-28

# Seahawks' Super Bowl Scores

## A Skilled Team

In 1983, Chuck Knox began coaching. With Knox, the team had many winning seasons. It kept winning more games than it lost. He led the team to its first AFC Championship game.

In 2006, the Seahawks went to its first Super Bowl. The team lost 10–21. In 2014, it played the big game again. That time, it won.

# CHAPTER 3

# Greatest

# MOMENTS

Seahawks' history is full of big moments. One of those was in a 1984 game. The Seahawks crushed the Kansas City Chiefs. It also made a record number of **pick-sixes**. The team's defense made six **interceptions**. Four of those interceptions became touchdowns. The Seahawks won 45–0.

Three different
Chiefs' quarterbacks
threw interceptions.

## Ending with an Interception

In 2014, the Seahawks played the San Francisco 49ers in the NFC Championship. During the fourth quarter, the Seahawks took the lead. But the 49ers battled the Seahawks, moving down the field. It looked like the 49ers could score. Then the Seahawks intercepted a pass. The team destroyed any hope for the 49ers.

# Winning in Overtime

In the 2015 NFC Championship, the Seahawks played the Green Bay Packers. The Packers led the entire game. With only minutes left, the Seahawks made two touchdowns. The team finally took the lead. A Packers' field goal tied the game. The Seahawks won in overtime.

Touchdown!

# BY THE NUMBERS

(as of 2018)

## 33%

**Super Bowl winning percentage**

## 5

**total retired jersey numbers**

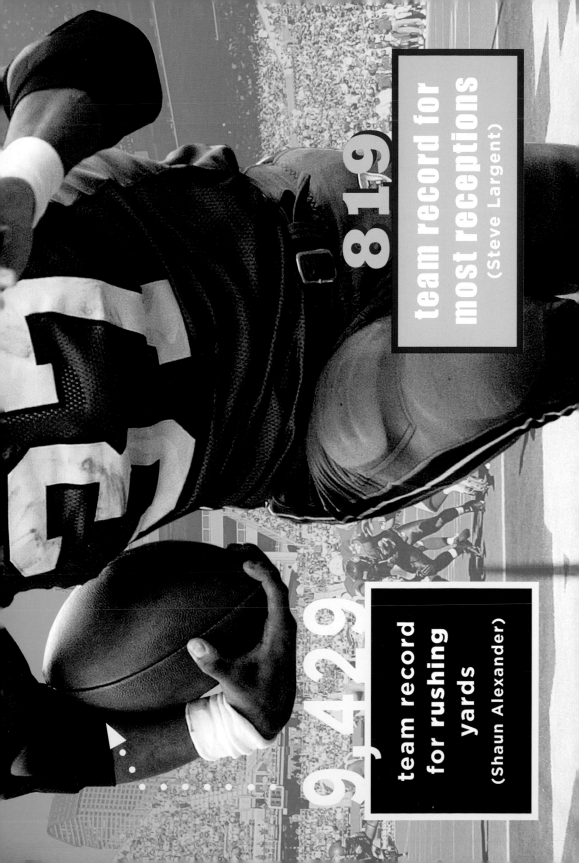

819
team record for
most receptions
(Steve Largent)

9,429
team record
for rushing
yards
(Shaun Alexander)

# CHAPTER 4

# STARS

## of the Seahawks

Many great players have worn Seahawks jerseys. Walter Jones played **offensive** tackle for the team. He plowed through defenders. In 1999, Jones became the Seahawks' first offensive lineman to make the Pro Bowl. He went nine times.

## Cortez Kennedy

Seahawks' defensive tackle Cortez Kennedy was strong and steady. Even though Kennedy was large, he was quick. He **dominated** the field using his size and strength. Kennedy was the 1992 Defensive Player of the Year.

# Largent's
# Records
## at Retirement

**177**
games in a row
## with a catch

career pass
## receptions
**819**

career receiving
## yards
**13,089**

career receiving
## touchdowns
**100**

# Steve Largent

Steve Largent joined the Seahawks in 1976. Largent wasn't the tallest or fastest wide receiver. But that didn't stop him. Largent caught 54 passes his rookie year. He retired as the all-time leading receiver.

# Comparing Some of the Seahawks' Coaches

The Seahawks has had several powerful coaches.

**Pete Carroll**

| | Pete Carroll |
|---|---|
| **years with team** | **9** |
| **win-loss-tie record** (including playoffs) | **98–60–1** |
| number of conference championship appearances | 2 |
| **Super Bowl appearances** (through 2018 season) | **2** |

PETE CARROLL

CHUCK KNOX

MIKE HOLMGREN

| Dennis Erickson | Mike Holmgren | Chuck Knox | Jack Patera |
|:---:|:---:|:---:|:---:|
| 4 | 10 | 9 | 7 |
| 31–33 | 90–80 | 83–67 | 35–59 |
| 0 | 1 | 1 | 0 |
| 0 | 0 | 0 | 0 |

DENNIS ERICKSON

JACK PATERA

## Shaun Alexander

Shaun Alexander played running back. He holds many team records. Alexander had a large part in the 2006 Super Bowl. He rushed for 95 yards. He was that season's league **MVP**.

### Most Single-Season Touchdowns by a Running Back

31 LaDainian Tomlinson

28 Shaun Alexander

27 Priest Holmes

26 Marshall Faulk

25 Emmitt Smith

(as of 2018 season)

# Marshawn Lynch

Marshawn Lynch played with the Seahawks from 2010 to 2015. With his powerful plays, he earned the nickname Beast Mode. He helped the team to many big wins.

## Kenny Easley

Kenny Easley was a star safety. He returned three interceptions for 155 yards his first year. He also recovered four fumbles. In 1984, he was the Defensive Player of the Year.

With amazing players and moments, the Seahawks has thrilled fans. They can't wait to see what the team does next.

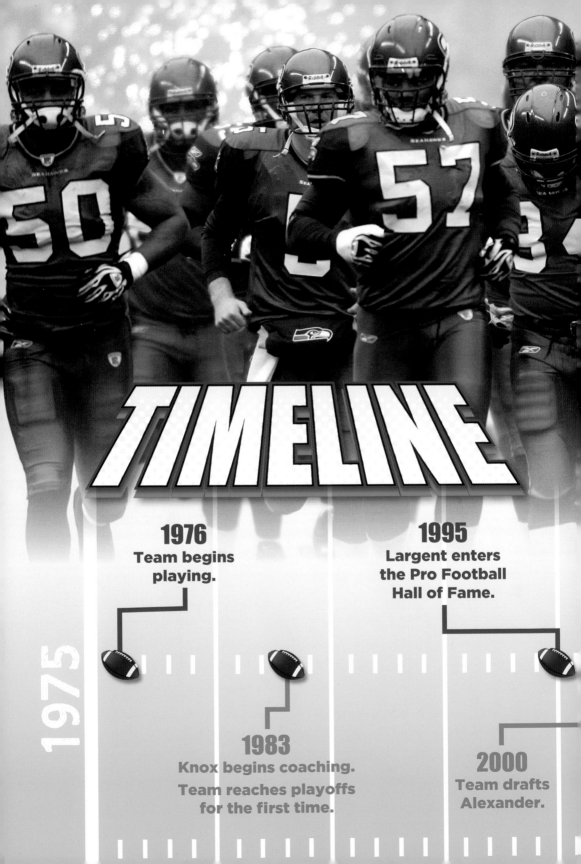

# TIMELINE

**1976**
Team begins playing.

**1995**
Largent enters the Pro Football Hall of Fame.

1975

**1983**
Knox begins coaching.
Team reaches playoffs for the first time.

**2000**
Team drafts Alexander.

**2006**
Team plays its first
Super Bowl.

**2015**
Team plays its
third Super Bowl.

**2014**
Seahawks win its
first Super Bowl.

**2017**
Easley enters the Pro
Football Hall of Fame.

2020

**defender** (de-FEN-dur)—a player who works to stop the other team from scoring

**dominate** (DOM-uh-neyt)—to hold a commanding position over

**interception** (in-tur-SEP-shun)—a catch made by a player from the opposing team

**MVP**—an award given to the best player in the league each season; MVP stands for most valuable player.

**offensive** (OH-fen-sive)—relating to the attempt to score in a game

**pick-six** (PIK-SIKS)—an interception returned for a touchdown; it stands for picking the ball from the other team and scoring six points.

**playoff** (PLAY-ahf)—a series of games played after the regular season to decide which player or team is the champion

**reception** (ree-SEP-shun)—catching a pass thrown toward the opponent's goal

**retire** (ree-TIYR)—to withdraw from use

**rushing** (RUSH-ing)—moving the football toward the goal using running plays

## BOOKS

**Cohn, Nate.** *Seattle Seahawks.* My First NFL Book. New York: AV2 by Weigl, 2018.

**Leventhal, Josh.** *Receivers.* Football's All-Time Greats. Mankato, MN: Black Rabbit Books, 2017.

**Morey, Allan.** *Superstars of the Seattle Seahawks.* Pro Sports Superstars NFL. Mankato, MN: Amicus, 2019.

## WEBSITES

Football: National Football League
**www.ducksters.com/sports/national_football_league.php**

Seahawks Official Team Website
**www.seahawks.com**

Seattle Seahawks Team Page
**www.nfl.com/teams/seattleseahawks/profile?team=SEA**

# INDEX